ИСТОРИЯ ЗА ЧИСЛАТА

THE NUMBER STORY

SMALL BOOK ONE

ENGLISH - BULGARIAN

Numbers Teach Children Their Number Names

written and illustrated by

MISS ANNA

Early Reader Edition of *The Number Story 1*
Bronze Medal Winner, 2016 Wishing Shelf Book Award

Cover by | Lumpy Publishing
Layout by | Lumpy Publishing
Translated by Iliana M.
Coloring by Jieeun Woo and Maria Mirabella

Library of Congress Control Number: 2018902040

Names: Miss Anna, author.
Title: Number story : numbers teach children their number names / Miss Anna.
Description: Portland, OR: Lumpy Publishing, 2018.
Identifiers: ISBN 978-1-945977-29-9 | LCCN 2018902040
Summary: The pictures and rhymes present stories which introduce numbers 0-10.
Subjects: LCSH Numeration—English--Bulgarian--Pictorial works--Juvenile literature. | BISAC JUVENILE NONFICTION /
Languages: English--Bulgarian
Classification: LCC QA141.3 .M57 2018 | DDC 513—dc23

Publisher: Lumpy Publishing
Website: www.missannabooks.com
Email: missanna@missannabooks.com

Paperback: ISBN 978-1-945977-29-9
Printed in the U.S.A. 1 3 5 7 9 10 8 6 4 2

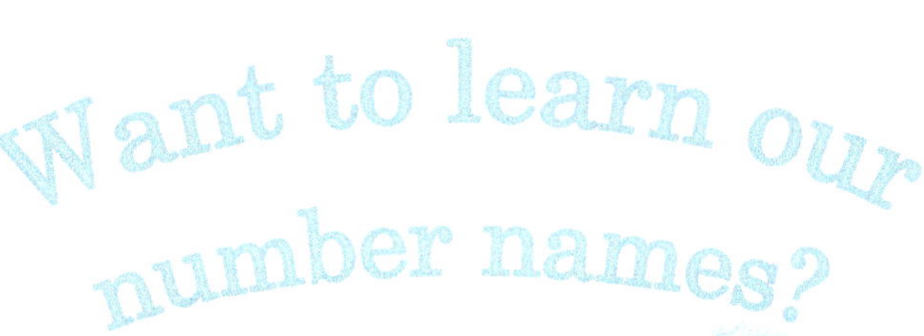

Искаш да научиш
имената на Числата?

It is very easy and a lot of fun!

Много е лесно и забавно!

Say-along our little jingle

Да попеем заедно.

starting from Number One!

Започваме от номер едно!

1

ONE looks like my one finger.

Едно

изглежда като моят един пръст.

ЕДНО!

2

TWO trails a tail.

Две

Има опашка.

A TAIL! ОПАШКА!

3

THREE has bumps.

Три

е като хълмове.

Хълмовете са неравен!

4

FOUR carries a sail.

Четири

е като платноходка.

Погледнете платната!

5

FIVE is a racing track.

Пет

е състезателна писта.

VROOM
БРЪЪЪМ!

SIX curves like a snail.

Шест

е с извивки като на охлюв.

A SNAIL! Охлюв!

7

SEVEN has a sharp angle.

Седем

Има остър ъгъл.

OUCH!
AY!

8

EIGHT is rollercoaster rails.

Осем

е като влакче на ужасите.

ЮПИИИИ!
YIPPEE!

NINE is a bubble on a stick.

Девет

е балонче върху пръчка.

A BUBBLE! БАЛОН!

10

TEN is an eye of a whale.

Десет

е око на кит.

WINK!

Намигва!

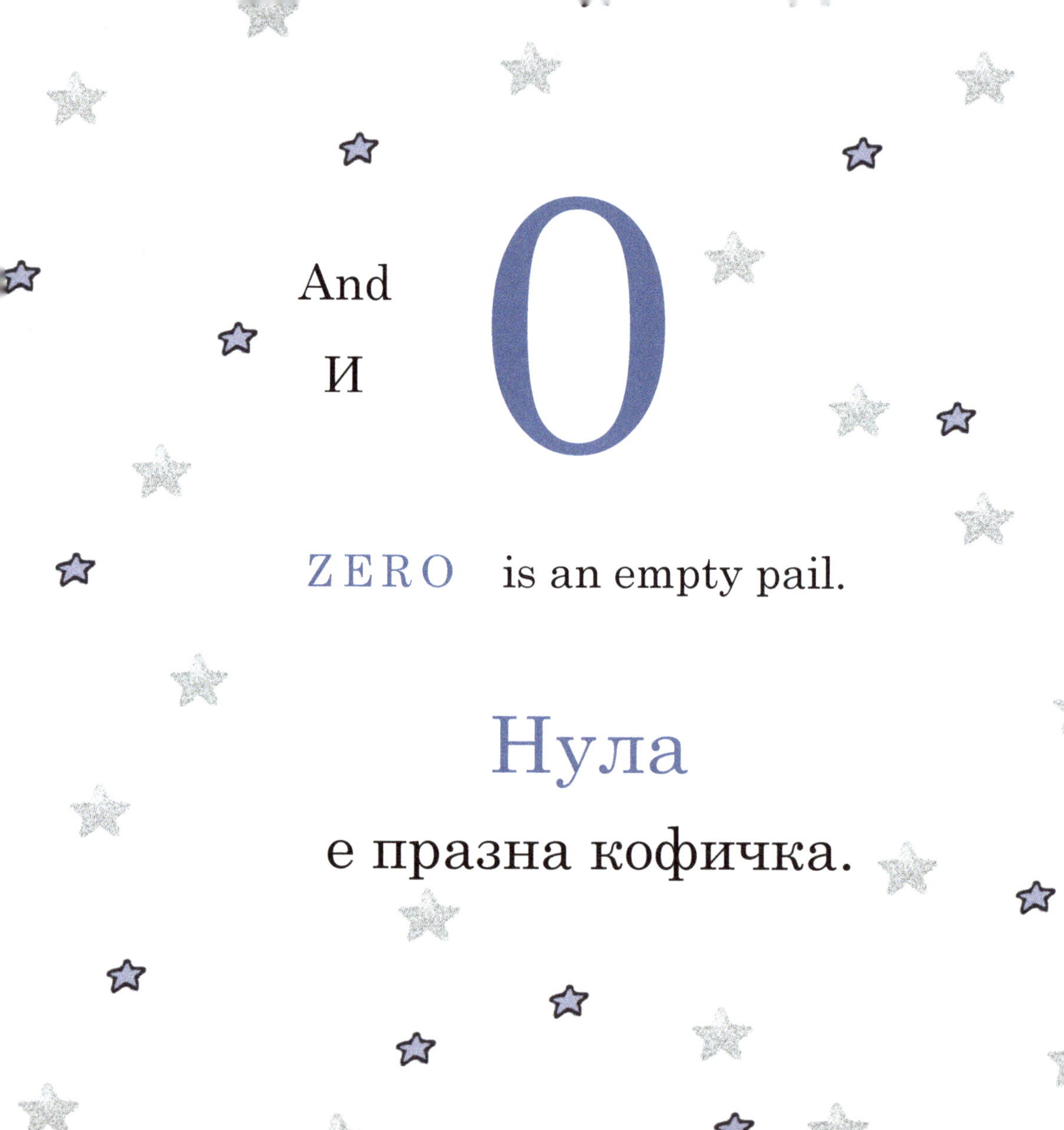

And
И

0

ZERO is an empty pail.

Нула
е празна кофичка.

IT'S EMPTY!

Празна е!

Thank you for playing with us today.

We had a lot of fun too!

Благодарим ти, че игра заедно с нас днес.

Ние също се забавлявахме!

We are your Number friends,
Zero to Ten,
Who will be here for you~

Ние сме твоите приятели Числата –
от Нула до Десет.
Ще бъдем тук специално за теб.

Bye-bye now!
See you again soon.

Чао за сега!
До скоро!

The Numbers are *SINGING* too!

To sing-a-long, look for Miss Anna Number Story

at your favorite music store like iTUNES.

MP3

Numbers 0-10
IDENTIFYING
& COUNTING

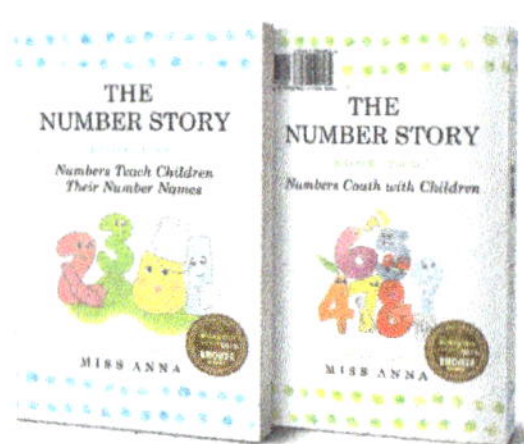

Number Story 1 & 2

isbn: 978-0-996216-48-7

Numbers 11-20 & Ordinals

first, second, third...

Number Story 3 & 4

isbn: 978-1-945977-01-5

Numbers 0-100 & Place Values

ones, tens, hundreds...

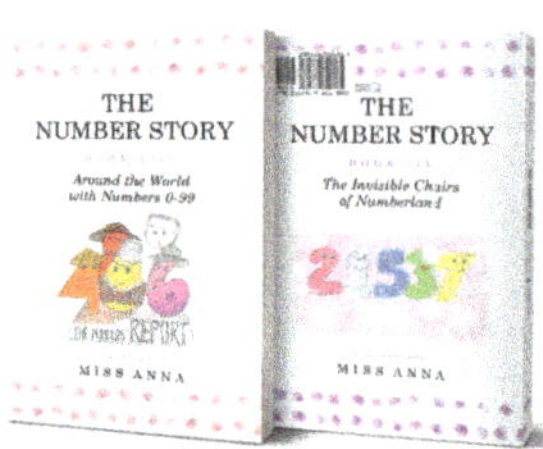

Number Story 5 & 6

isbn: 978-1-945977-06-0

About Clocks & Telling Time

hours, minutes, seconds

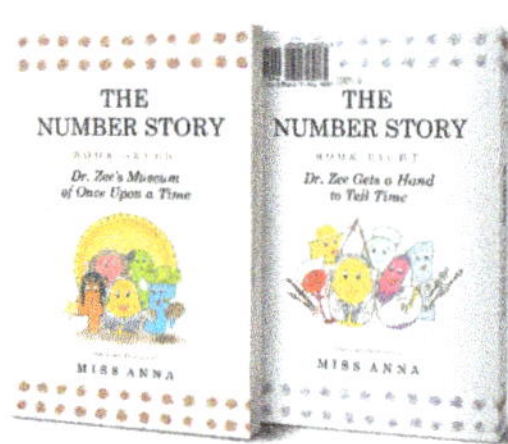

Number Story 7 & 8

isbn: 978-1-949320-40-4

For more Miss Anna books to love,
visit us at

www.missannabooks.com

Numbers are working hard all over the world!
Come Travel the World with Us!

www.ingramcontent.com/pod-product-compliance
Ingram Content Group UK Ltd.
Pitfield, Milton Keynes, MK11 3LW, UK
UKHW061949290726
14090UKWH00021B/1146

9 781945 977299